Some of Each

*A Definitively Preliminary
Super-Half-Mini Tome
of
"Indulgently" Tasty Bites*

Or

*25ish Irreverent Recipes with
Semi-Infinite Possibilities*

Cheryl Wheeler

Copyright © 2017 Cheryl Wheeler

All rights reserved.

ISBN-13: 978-1976562310

DEDICATION

To gluten. May you always remain digestible.

CONTENTS

	Introduction	1
1	**Mornings**	**5**
	Cardamom Semolina Cereal	6
	WTH is Puttu	8
	Yummy Pancakes: Banana Nutmeg Version	11
	Yummy Pancakes: Sweet Potato-Carrot Version	13
	Delish Fruit Sauce for Your Pancake Extravaganza	15
2	**Mid-Days**	**16**
	Empanada Dough	17
	"Mostly Peas" Samosas	19
	Cheryl's Chinese-Japanese-Thai Veggie Gyozas	22
	Two Insane Egg Curries	24
	Meaty Gyozas (Taiwanese Style)	29
	My Own Pork Pozole	31
3	**Afternoons**	**34**
	"In My Own Dojo" Ice Cream	36
	Persian Ice Cream	38
	Chicha Morada (Peruvian Purple Corn Drink)	40

Inexact Watermelon-Ade Smoothie	42
My Own "Greek" Sweet Brioche Bread	43
Many Options Drunken Figs	46
Highly Versatile Beany Chocolate Chip Cookies	48
Just Yummy (Banana Peanut Butter Chocolate Chip Cookies)	50

4   Evenings   51

Red Cabbage Goodness	52
Shalloty Goodness Salad Dressing	54
Spanish Lentil-Parsley Salad	55
Sri Lankan Carrot Salad	57
Yum Sin (Noodle Salad), My Way	59
Sourdough Pizza for a Crowd	61
Whole Potato Pizza Crusts	65
Disconcerting Inverted Field Roast Pizza	68
A SOUP TO END ALL SOUPS	70
Lazy-Healthy-Easy Soup Cheat	74

The Wrap Up   **75**

ACKNOWLEDGMENT

The existence of this modest paperback book would not have been possible without the trees upon which it is printed. IOU big time.

INTRODUCTION

Welcome, curious cook! I applaud your adventurous spirit in purchasing this book. Let's dive in.

About me. I have been cooking and experimenting with food since I could stand on a chair to reach the countertop as a grubby little kid. The chemistry of food and how foods transform through heat, particularly in baking, is truly fascinating.

But of course, eating something delicious is the most fascinating part. I am mostly interested in new and unusual flavors. Even so, as I experiment over the years I have found that there are some favorites that I always come back to even though they are no longer unusual to me. This small book is perhaps the first (or last, depending on my overall gumption) in a series of books where I attempt to organize some of my more successful cooking thoughts and experiments in one place for others to ponder at their own risk.

To keep my neophile's palate entertained, I have done some enlightening food-themed travels on several continents. I always try to take advantage of cooking opportunities and lessons whenever possible. I lived and worked for several years in Thailand, where I developed a deep appreciation for umami and a love of constant snacking (probably the most popular Thai "hobby" –just ask the Thais!). I hope to continue to do much more of this traveling and living abroad in the future as well. While many of the recipes in this book come from ideas gathered while traveling, some of the others come from ideas gathered while traveling in my mind, through films, documentaries, books, reading cookbooks and talking to and cooking with intriguing people from other places.

As a mom to a now-teenaged kiddo, Evan, I have had the opportunity to test these recipes on him and receive the kind of honest feedback you can only get from your offspring. He's not a supertaster (look it up if you're not sure what this is) and he is an adventurous eater, but he has always had reliably high standards. Trust us both when we say this stuff is yummy.

I love thinking about cooking sometimes more than actually cooking, and I can be found reading cookbooks for fun at random hours of the night. But I admit that writing about it feels a tad wind-baggy. For this reason, I resist including luscious foreplay-like detailed introductions that I see on some cooking blogs these days. I'd like to get to the point already. Persnicketiness about these creative conflicts may come through a bit in these pages. I may regret that later, but I doubt it.

A note on content. I call this book *Some of Each* because it represents a smattering of the recipes I've worked out over the last few years. Maybe another time I can focus on more specific genres, but this time I'm into sharing a bit of variety. Regarding ingredient choices, I'm big on plain fresh fruits and high quality plain fresh vegetables, I am slightly less big into breads and other carbs, even more slightly less into desserts, and I am not heavily into meats. All this means if you're a fruit lover, don't despair because I don't talk as incessantly about fruit here as I would in person. Just eat fruit. If you're a meat lover, the same goes for you, don't despair, I am sure you can find your savory solace elsewhere.

A note on measurements. Where it's OK to be imprecise (which is in most cases *except for bread, cakes and pastries*), I speak in cups and such, but I do measure some ingredients in grams when it really, really matters—in bread, cakes and pastries! It is critical to use a scale for consistent results. And I use grams because they are fantastically easy to calculate. Wouldn't you rather calculate by 10s 100s and 1,000s than by 12th or 16ths or whatever the f**k Imperial crap is about? Suck it up and use a scale.

There are plenty of great scales and detailed reviews of their pros and cons all over the Internet. I use a glass-top digital scale, but you only need to get one that you can handle mentally and aesthetically—and one that you can clean easily. You might also want to choose one that fits whatever bowls and plates and containers you'll be using when cooking. That said, despite my love of the metric system, you'll also see I mention inches in these recipes, because, hey, I just think in inches because I currently live in the US. Look up *Why Won't America Go Metric? Our Centuries-Long Ambivalence About Our Place in the World* by John Bemelmans Marciano if you're interested.

A note on the overall organization of this mini tome. Organization is a beast. Since these recipes represent a modest selection and they should all appear neatly in the table of contents, I didn't include an index.

Hopefully an indexless cookbook will not cause you as much angst as they typically cause me.

You'll see that I grouped the recipes by time of day rather than by type of food. Even so, I don't believe there is a right or a wrong time to eat certain foods. I am a serious fan of dinner leftovers for breakfast or breakfast for dinner. I am also a big fan of the *I will eat whatever the hell I want to eat today* diet plan. Essentially, I needed a general pattern, and recommended times for noshing—recommended for your maximum pleasure—seemed like an OK approach. Think, with your taste buds, about what sounds good to both you and them, then go from there. Each recipe will serve 2-4 people and/or will provide you with exciting intentional, or non-intentional but welcome, leftovers.

Finally, hey, what about photos? I enjoy photography, and I thought carefully about including photos, but then realized that if I spent my time taking and editing photos for this book, it just wouldn't happen. Furthermore, this book was originally written to publish on Kindle and I personally have an ancient black and white e-reader that doesn't show pictures very well, so, for my fellow e-book-reading semi-luddites out there, I thoughtfully spared them from the visual clutter. But for those of you buying this book in paperback form, use your friggin' imagination (or the Internet).

1 MORNINGS

It is difficult to say what one should *really* be eating in the morning, but let's hope it's food. I understand we all have our attachments to what one's taste buds should experience in the morning. What I have included here are just a few things that I find acceptable and I assume other people would probably also find acceptable.

My various pancake recipes have been popular with both kids and adults so I encourage you to try those first if you have any doubts. There was one point where I considered writing a cookbook that contained only one recipe. That would be my pancake recipe.

Cardamom Semolina Cereal

Way tastier than oatmeal but probably not as healthy, so take your vitamins.

INGREDIENTS

1 cup semolina
2 tablespoons cultured butter
1 teaspoon salt
2 ¼ cups whole milk
¼ teaspoon whole black cardamom seeds, crushed and chopped finely
1 tablespoon jaggery or dark brown sugar
¼ cup sliced toasted almonds or toasted chopped cashews (or both)
¼ cup golden raisins, dried cherries, dried cranberries, or dark raisins or any combination of these*
Sprinkle of cinnamon or fresh grated nutmeg or both or neither
More salt, butter, sugar and milk, to taste

DIRECTIONS

Heat a nonstick skillet over medium heat, then add the semolina and stir with a spatula. The semolina will not turn brown but will seem a little bit toasted. Add the butter and stir around with the spatula to cook a little bit more. Next, add the salt and then the milk. Stir and you will see the semolina getting clumpy but keep stirring and it will start to get smooth. It is absorbing the milk, nomnom. Throw in the cardamom, sugar, nuts, and dried fruits. Stir. You may need to add a little more milk, sugar and salt, or other spices to your liking. It depends on your preferences, so taste and discover. Eat this like you'd eat oatmeal. Alternatively, you can pat it into a buttered dish and let it get firm, then slice it up and eat it in breakfasty squares.

NOTE

There are some interesting and popular savory versions of this dish made with onions, chilies, curry leaves and veggies. They are called exciting things such as "upma rava" and are worth looking into!

*Feeling crazy? Try barberries (very sour!) or maybe even some diced candied citrus here.

Cheryl Wheeler

WTH is Puttu

Do you like salty rice? Do you like fresh unsweetened coconut? Give this South Indian steamed rice "bread" a stab.

INGREDIENTS

2 cups raw red rice
1 ½ teaspoons salt
1 cup fresh grated coconut (NO sugary or dried stuff, use real fresh coconut)
Pandan leaf (1 is more than enough)*
Water

DIRECTIONS

Soak the rice in enough water to cover well, overnight. Drain the water and spread the rice on a kitchen towel to dry for a few minutes (5 minutes has been sufficient for me).

Grind the rice in batches in a blender or whatever grinding device you have handy until it is mildly coarse, such that perhaps each grain of rice seems to be broken into 5-6 pieces. Don't bother trying to get it into an ultra-fine powder.

In a large bowl, combine the ground rice, salt and 4 tablespoons of the grated coconut. Start sprinkling water *very, very stingily* onto the rice mixture and stir to combine. Use your hands so you can feel you're getting the right amount of water.

What is the right amount of water? When you squeeze it, it will hold together, but then it will crumble. You don't want to get it any wetter than that.

Grab that puttu mold* that you bought but haven't used in a while and start just the steamer portion on medium-high heat to get some water boiling on the stovetop.

Flat in the bottom of the puttu mold; put a little square of pandan leaf. Then put 1-2 tablespoons of shredded coconut on top of that. Top that with spoonfuls of the rice and coconut mixture until it reaches half-way up the mold. Put in 2 tablespoons coconut, then fill to just about the top of the mold with rice, and top that with another 1-2 tablespoons of shredded coconut. The reason for the coconut in the middle is so you can easily divide the log into two loglets to share each puttu unit with a non-questioning friend.

Steam the mold on the top of the steamer for 10 minutes on high heat. Now use a chopstick to gently push the log out of the puttu mold onto a plate.

This recipe will make about 3ish puttu logs in a normal sized puttu mold.

Eat puttu with sliced ripe bananas and jaggery or brown sugar for breakfast or with any spicy curry of your choice! My favorite is Sri Lankan egg curry (fortunately included in this super-half-mini tome). Puttu is also incredibly tasty warmed up and then sprinkled on top of vanilla or pandan ice cream.

*What is it? *Pandanus amaryllifolius*. Look it up.

**Give up and throw it all away right now if you don't have a puttu mold.* Just kidding. If you don't have one, you can line a flat-bottomed steamer basket with muslin, then put a few bits of pandan leaf on top of the muslin, and pour your rice-coconut mixture in there. Steam for about 10 minutes. It will be crumbly and non-log-shaped, but the taste will be the same.

EXCITING VARIATION

Replace one cup of the ground red rice with one cup of commercial white or brown rice flour, but add the flour after you have ground the red rice, when you are stirring in the salt. Add miniscule amounts of water to dry mixture until it *just* clumps together in your hand. Adding the commercial flour will make the puttu more bread-like and less rice-like. Note that you CANNOT be sloppy about the amount of water you add when you use flour, because too much water will result in a gluey, nasty textured puttu.

Yummy Pancakes: Banana Nutmeg Version

One of Evan's fifth grade friends randomly shouted at school one day, "You know who makes the best pancakes!? Evan's mom!" Trust the experts.

INGREDIENTS

<u>Wet things</u>
1 cup full fat Greek yogurt
½ cup whole milk
½ cup ricotta cheese
¼ cup water
3 large eggs
1 large ripe banana

<u>Dry things</u>
1 ½ cups white whole wheat flour
½ cup coconut flour (½ cup whole wheat is also OK)
2 tablespoons raw (turbinado) sugar*
1 teaspoon salt
1 teaspoon baking soda
4 teaspoons baking powder
2-3 gratings of whole nutmeg
4 tablespoons butter (¼ cup or "half a stick"), cut into small cubes

DIRECTIONS

Smoosh up the wet things in a bowl, starting with the bananas, then the eggs, then the rest.

Mix dry things together. Add the butter to the dry stuff and smash it between your fingers into the dry stuff so it makes little balls the size of fat peas.

Heat up the griddle to 375°F.

Mix the wet things into the dry – don't stir too long! Over-stirring makes pancakes sad.

When the griddle is hot, either rub it with oil (like coconut oil or canola oil) or spray it with an oil spray like canola oil spray. Use a ⅓ cup measure to plop the pancake batter onto the hot griddle and spread them out a little to be the thickness you like if they don't want to spread.

Watch the pancakes cook. They will start to look like they're getting dry. They will get bubbles on top. When the bottoms look dry and your spatula can scoot under them without getting batter stuck on it, you can carefully or boldly flip them over. This is where it pays off to have the pancakes be a bit small so they'll be easier to flip.

*The more sugar you add, the greater risk of the pancakes getting dark/burned. Sugar burns fairly fast. Consider the fact that there is also sugar in the bananas!

Yummy Pancakes: Sweet Potato-Carrot Version

Non-secret note: this happens to be totally gluten free, but tastes good. A little more work than the banana version, but worthwhile. Consider doubling the batch and freezing some for later.

INGREDIENTS

<u>Wet things</u>
2 ½ cups whole milk and/or whole milk mixed with Greek yogurt (1 cup Greek yogurt, the rest milk)
3 large eggs
1 teaspoon apple cider vinegar
2 tablespoons golden flax meal
1 medium sized washed carrot (about ½ cup), roughly chopped
1 cup steamed white sweet potato, including peel

<u>Dry things</u>
2 cups of a variety of gluten free flours:
—½ cup white rice flour
—½ cup fine cornmeal
—½ cup teff flour
—½ cup coconut flour
2 tablespoons raw (turbinado) sugar*
1 ½ teaspoons salt
1 teaspoon baking soda
4 teaspoons baking powder
Few small gratings of nutmeg
4 tablespoons butter (¼ cup or half a stick), cut into small cubes

DIRECTIONS

In a blender, mix wet things together. Toss in the carrots and sweet potato and blend for a long while. Let it sit while you do the dry things. Letting it sit allows the flax to moisten up which eventually helps, with the eggs, to bind the pancakes together very nicely sans gluten.

Mix dry things together. Add the butter to the dry stuff and smash it between your fingers into the dry stuff so it makes little balls the size of fat peas. This probably isn't necessary but it is fun and tactile. If you don't want to stick your hands in your pancake batter, melt the butter, cool it, and slowly stir the cooled melted butter into the dry stuff.

Whir the blender again for a bit.

Heat up the griddle to 375°F.

Whir blender again. Mix the wet things into the dry— it's OK to stir it clumsily, or, uh, "well." Since there is no gluten, these puppies won't get tough due to over-stirring—WOW!

When the griddle is hot, either rub it with oil (like coconut oil or canola oil) or spray it with an oil spray like canola oil spray. Use a ⅓ cup measure to plop the pancake batter onto the hot griddle and spread them out a little to be the thickness you like if they don't want to spread.

Watch the pancakes cook. The bottoms will start to look like they're getting dry. They will get bubbles on top but not a ton. When the bottoms look dry, you can carefully or boldly flip them over. This is where it pays off to have the pancakes be a bit small so they'll be easier to flip.

*The more sugar you add, the greater risk of things getting dark/burned. Sugar burns fairly fast. Consider the fact that there is also sugar in the carrots and sweet potato.

Delish Fruit Sauce
For Your Pancake Extravaganza

Or fruit "syrup" if you want to call it that.

INGREDIENTS

1 cup frozen fruit (blueberries are especially nice, but please experiment!)
1-2 tablespoons water
4 drops liquid stevia
Dash of sea salt

DIRECTIONS

Cook fruit in microwave with water for about 3 minutes, until soft. Make sure you microwave it in a big enough glass bowl or large glass measuring cup so that it won't explode all over the inside of the microwave!

Add stevia, dash of salt, then put in blender for 30-60 seconds until thoroughly liquefied.

If you don't like seeds in your syrup, push the mush through a fine strainer with a silicon spatula to get most of the seeds out.

Serve in a nice syrup dispenser so it feels classy. And be generous when you pour it on your pancakes!

2 MID-DAYS

Here we are going to get into some savory tidbits.

As a nerd for things found inside doughy pockets, I have included four pocket-like recipes here. Two of which are gyozas because I am slightly crazy about gyozas. I am just microscopically slightly less crazy about empanadas and samosas. I could go on and on about the versatility of empanadas but that would leave me nothing to say for the next mini tome, now wouldn't it?

I have included some of my favorite proteiny items here as well, and this is because I think it is most comfortable to eat heavy foods in the middle of the day. You may disagree but you also may be too lazy to make these things at a different time. I know how you are.

Sorry-not-sorry to the vegs and vegans about the hard-core pork pozole recipe. I suspect you could use other substances instead, but I taught myself to make it with pork and I really do think you get the maximum sin for your buck with the pork.

Empanada Dough

Good times! A touch of white whole wheat flour keeps these babies sassy.

INGREDIENTS
200 grams all-purpose flour
70 grams white whole wheat flour
1 ½ teaspoons kosher salt
57 grams very cold unsalted butter, cut into small cubes
51 grams very cold leaf lard or vegetable shortening, cut/scooped into small pieces
1 large egg
78 grams ice water
1 tablespoon distilled white vinegar (just replace with water if you're making a sweet filling)

DIRECTIONS

Stir flours with salt in a large bowl and smash in the two fats with your fingertips or a pastry blender until mixture resembles coarse meal with some (roughly pea-size) fat lumps.

Mix together egg, ice water, and vinegar in a bowl with a fork. Add to flour mixture, stirring with fork until just incorporated. (They say the dough looks shaggy at this point, and indeed this is true).

Turn the dough out onto a lightly floured surface and gather together, then knead gently only a few times, just enough to bring dough together. You want to still see the fat lumps in the dough but the dough is smooth overall. Form dough into a flattened rectangle and chill, wrapped in plastic wrap, at least 1 hour.

This dough should still be nice and pliable after chilling. Cut in half to work with a reasonably sized piece and roll out on surface well dusted with flour. You can get it rolled out somewhere between ⅛ and ¼ inch thick. Use a pastry bench scraper as needed to keep dough from sticking. Use a large (4-5-inch diameter) biscuit cutter to cut them out.*

Fill with some reasonable amount of filling. There are infinite possibilities for fillings—use the Internet AND your imagination—or just be understandably lazy and see my *Mostly Peas Samosas* recipe in this book. To shape empanadas, fold them over, dab edge with water lightly, squeeze shut, and crimp with your fingers or smush together with the tines of a fork. There are tons of sexy videos online that will show you how to strategize for optimal empanada shaping.

Prior to baking, you can brush the empanadas with melted lard, melted butter or with a beaten egg (egg wash) for additional entertainment.

Baking at 400°F seems reasonable. Maybe 12-20 minutes depending on the size of the pockets you build. Keep an eye on them so they bake up golden brown and yum.

*Super groovy lazy cheater's option: Roll out each half of the dough into a big rectangle about 11ish x 17ish inches, put filling on one side and fold over then seal, making two massive long empanadas out of each piece! Doing it this way takes about 30 minutes of baking at 400°F. Just cut them up (after they've cooled) and eat like sandwiches.

"Mostly Peas" Samosas

In a quest to squeeze more vegetables into savory items, I came up with this mostly peas samosa recipe in which the potatoes primarily function to hold all the peas together.

I lean toward the larger amounts of spices here, but you can do less—or more.

INGREDIENTS
1 cup yellow potatoes (Yukon Gold are nice), or other cute, dense potato with thin skins, chopped up
1 tablespoon mild oil (canola, perhaps)
1-2 teaspoons black mustard seeds
1-2 teaspoons coriander seed, crushed
1-2 teaspoons cumin seed, crushed
⅓ cup finely chopped onion (red ones are neat)
1-2 teaspoons grated fresh ginger
1-2 red Thai mouse turd chilies*, chopped finely
2 ¼ cups frozen green peas
⅓ cup very finely chopped fresh cilantro, stems and all
1 teaspoon salt
1 teaspoon garam masala
1 teaspoon amchoor (dried mango powder)
2 teaspoons lemon or lime juice

1-2 teaspoons ajwain seeds
A batch of dough that works for building pockets**

DIRECTIONS

Boil the potatoes (remember to use water) for 20 minutes until they are tender. Drain, then smash up. Just leave on the skins, they're gonna keep your samosas more fun.

Heat the oil over medium heat, add the mustard seeds, coriander and cumin, then fry just briefly until they smell good. Add the onion and ginger, then cook and stir until the onions are looking soft. Add the potatoes and cook, stirring for some minutes until everything looks like it is getting, well, cooked. Take off the heat, stir in the peas and the chopped cilantro. Add the spices. Toss in the lemon or lime juice. Cool for a few minutes, then make more spice adjustments. You might want to increase the spiciness or saltiness, it is up to you. You might even want to throw in a little sugar if that feels right. †

Now I will tell you a crazy non-secret (just in case you skipped to the end of this recipe). You can use my empanada dough recipe to make nice samosas! Just add a teaspoon of ajwain seeds (fruits, technically) to the empanada dough when you add the water/eggs/vinegar to change up the flavor! Or, if you forget, just pat the ajwain into the dough when you're rolling it out.

I will almost always bake samosas rather than deep-fry. You can deep fry them if you want but I will not lead you astray into the rough terrain of deep-frying. This is how I bake them:

Heat your oven to 400°F.

Follow some great online directions from somebody cool such as Andrea Nguyen or any number of lovely Indian YouTube grandmas regarding how to shape samosas. Essentially what you do is create a little cone with the dough, hold it in one paw and fill it as full as you can with the filling, then fold the dough over and seal. But please observe how it is done before proceeding.

After you've done that fun stuff, put the samosas on a baking sheet that has been lined with parchment paper, brush them with melted butter or ghee if you know how to make (or buy!) ghee.

Bake the samosas for about 15 minutes, then turn them over, brush with more butter and bake on the other side 10-15 minutes more. Or more! Keep an eye on them! You want them to come out of the oven golden and brown, not pale and sickly.

SOME of EACH

*Yes, this a real thing.

**If using my empanada dough recipe doesn't sit well with you for some reason, or you just want to try something different, I generally approve of the pastry for Alton Brown's *Pocket Pies* recipe. It is sturdy and tasty, although when I use it, I always end up replacing half the shortening with butter. I sometimes use my sourdough pizza dough and make kind of a calzone-samosa hybrid.

†Are you already bored? Just let the filling cool and then eat. Call it spicy potato-pea salad!

Cheryl's Chinese-Japanese-Thai Veggie Gyozas

Conceptually filched from a taciturn Chinese alcoholic who lived in Japan then moved to Thailand to hone his stellar craft in quiet desperation.

INGREDIENTS

Package of good quality gyoza wrappers*

1 cup finely diced shiitake mushroom caps, soaked in very hot water until soft (please squeeze the water out)
2 glass noodle bundles, soaked in very hot water for about 5-6 minutes, then drained, cooled and chopped very small
1 carrot, very finely grated
4 cups very finely chopped green cabbage
2 tablespoons finely chopped green onions
2 tablespoons mirin (or find a substitute online)
2 tablespoons low-sodium soy sauce
2 teaspoons peeled and grated fresh ginger
½ teaspoon salt
½ teaspoon sugar
1 teaspoon dark sesame oil
3 garlic cloves, minced

DIRECTIONS

Mix all filling ingredients together in a bowl!** You can taste the filling to see if you like it. Adjust the flavorings as you prefer. Things not working out? Contemplate MSG.

Take a scant tablespoon of the filling, spoon it off-center in a gyoza wrapper, then fold over the wrapper and seal with water. Pinch the ends together and pinch all along the edge to create a nice design. If you can stand it, please observe how this is done via some good online videos before proceeding. Put the finished gyoza on parchment paper as you make them they'll be ready when you are ready to fry them up in batches.

Heat some canola or peanut oil in a large non-stick frying pan over medium-high heat. Fry the gyoza until their bottoms are brown. Now pour a small amount of water (about ¼ cup) into the pan and cover tightly right away. You should then cook (steam) them for about 8 minutes or until gyozas appear to be cooked through. The water will have evaporated and the base of the dumplings are golden and can be lifted from the pan with a spatula. Move the gyozas around in the pan and let them cook a bit more until they are dry. At this point, I like to fry on all three sides for a crispier outer texture, but it's not necessary.

Serve with a dipping sauce of your choice. I like this (relatively popular) one well enough:

⅓ cup rice vinegar
¼ cup chopped green onions
¼ cup low-sodium soy sauce
½ teaspoon crushed red pepper

*Sometimes I make my own dough, it's easy, it just adds time. Enlist your current would-be lover to assist you if time feels like a problem. I recommend the Extra Chewy Dough version of the Basic Dumpling Dough recipe from *Asian Dumplings* by Andrea Nguyen.

**Getting bored already? Eat as-is! Call it salad!

Two Insane Egg Curries

What I love about these recipes is the extra-complicated format makes getting through either of these (actually simple) dishes feel like an exotic accomplishment.

Option A: Burmese
Option B: Sri Lankan

INGREDIENTS

For A & B:

6 large eggs
Splash of white vinegar

Option A: Burmese Egg Curry INGREDIENTS

¼ cup peanut oil
¼ teaspoon fresh turmeric
1 curry leaf
1 large shallot (¼-ish cup), finely minced
3 cloves garlic, finely minced
½ teaspoon red chili powder
Two large *excellent quality in-season* tomatoes, finely chopped
2 tablespoons fish sauce
2 teaspoons salt
4 jalapeno peppers, seeded and sliced in halves

Note that you can adjust the spices up or down, but what I've written here is going to be tasty by my standards.

DIRECTIONS

Option A & B: Proper Hard Boiled Eggs

Put eggs in a small saucepan and add cold water just barely to cover. Throw just a splash of white vinegar into the pot. Cook at medium-high heat until the water starts to boil, turn the heat down just to medium and cover the pot and boil, gently, for nine minutes. Drain the eggs, rinse with cold water and soak in ice-cold water for about 10 minutes to cool down. When they are cool enough to peel, do so.

Option A: Burmese Egg Curry DIRECTIONS

Heat the peanut oil in a small non-stick skillet over medium-high heat. When oil is hot enough to sizzle when a curry leaf is dropped into it, add the turmeric and stir once, then add the peeled eggs and roll them around gently, frying them until they look like fried tofu all over. Aim to fry them evenly, as it makes them look and feel good, but don't beat yourself up if they're a tad uneven. Carefully lift the eggs out of the hot oil with an appropriate tool and let them cool.

Pour the turmeric-laden oil into a larger frying pan and add the shallots and garlic. Fry these guys on medium heat until they are translucent. Next add the tomatoes and chili powder. Add the sliced peppers. Stir this well to keep it from sticking and cook it at a decent simmer until the tomatoes are broken down and the pepper bits look soft enough to be tasty to you. This could take about 10 or 12 minutes depending on how mushy your tomatoes are to begin with.

Add fish sauce and salt, stir for a moment to blend. Turn heat down to low.

Cut the eggs as neatly as possible into quarters or halves, then place the eggs into the sauce gently, yolk side up. Cook the eggs and sauce gently on low heat until everything is warm. Carefully serve hot or at room temperature with rice. This is decent a bit cold, too, you just need to feel good about it.

Option B: Sri Lankan Egg Curry INGREDIENTS

½ cup canola oil
1 large red onion (1 cup or more), chopped small
4 garlic cloves, roughly chopped
1 tablespoon Maldive fish flakes*, ground (it's OK to substitute 1 tablespoon fish sauce!)
1-2-inch piece of a real Ceylon cinnamon stick*
2-inch piece pandan leaf**
1 ½ teaspoon cumin seeds, toasted
2 teaspoons red chili powder
4 mild to medium hot green chilies, such jalapeno, finely chopped
3-4 red Thai mouse turd chilies†, whole or split (if you like—packs a nice punch)
1 full sprig of curry leaves††, leaves picked off, stem discarded
2 cups of coconut milk (or coconut cream if you're going hard-core)
1 teaspoon grated fresh or dry turmeric
1 ½ teaspoons salt (or to taste)

1-3 cups multi-colored carrots, julienned and lightly steamed
2 cups fresh cilantro leaves, washed and dried (no need to chop)
All the stems of the cilantro leaves, finely chopped

Option B: Sri Lankan Egg Curry DIRECTIONS

Heat the canola oil in a small non-stick skillet over medium-high heat. When oil is hot enough to sizzle when a curry leaf is dropped into it, you may add the peeled eggs to the oil, in batches (so as not to reduce the overall heat of the oil too much) and roll them around and fry them until they look fried like tofu all over. Yes, the goal is to fry them all over and make them cute but again don't beat yourself up if they're a tad uneven. The real benefit to frying them this way is that the texture holds onto more of the curry sauce. Carefully lift the eggs out of the hot oil with chopsticks or a slotted spoon and let them cool.

Using some of the oil from the egg frying (or, hey, starting over with coconut oil is OK too if you're into it, but it's not worth it in most cases, since you will get the coconut flavor from the coconut milk), fry the red onion and garlic on medium heat. Fry these guys until they are translucent. Then add the various chilies, stir for a minute or two, and add the rest of the ingredients through the salt (please save the carrots and cilantro for serving time, they will turn to mush if you add them now!). Simmer and stir all that on low heat for 15ish minutes, adding a little water as you watch it to keep it the consistency you prefer. Add the eggs and gently simmer on even lower heat for 15 minutes longer.

Pour that nice stuff in a serving bowl. If you're bothered by those hulking eggs, you do have the option to pluck them out and slice them in half or quarters so they look cute. I think they look nice sliced in the dish but your hands are likely to protest the heat; proceed with caution. And if you are saving it for later (and yes it tastes very nice the next day!) I say leave the eggs whole and slice later.

After you've addressed your egg aesthetics, generously top the bowl of curry with the steamed carrots and even more generously with the cilantro leaves and stems. Have more cilantro and carrots at the table as a balance to the richness of the curry itself.

You are required to serve this curry at least once with *WTH is Puttu*.

*Dried Skipjack tuna rocks, in a nutshell, for a uniquely Sri Lankan umami blast. Fish sauce is an OK substitute but you can order Maldive fish online so you don't have a ton of excuses.

** through †† These tasties are worth buying at the Asian grocery and holding onto as they will all stick around—the Maldive fish doesn't require any refrigeration and the pandan leaves, mouse turd chilies and curry leaves can all be frozen whole, the frozen bits easily chopped or snipped off when needed. And yes, Thai mouse turd chilies are a real thing.

Meaty Gyozas (Taiwanese Style)

A generously large Taiwanese family recipe gathered from the foodie world, replete with freedom (i.e. your creative freedom).

INGREDIENTS

2 packages of good quality gyoza wrappers*

230 grams of each of the following:
- Chopped frozen spinach
- Ground pork
- Ground chicken meat
- Chopped fresh shrimp

6 or 7 dried shiitake mushroom caps (be sure to not use any stems), soaked, squeezed and chopped
2 stalks of chopped green onions
A generous pinch of fresh grated ginger
A splash of roasted sesame oil
White pepper to taste
Oil for pan-frying

DIRECTIONS

Mix all ingredients together.

Take a scant tablespoon of the filling, spoon it off-center in a gyoza wrapper, then fold over the wrapper and seal with water. Pinch the ends together. If you can stand it, please observe how this is done via some good online videos before proceeding.

Wrap and pan-fry just one or two dumplings to try the flavor, if the flavor isn't what you like, add more to the filling of what you think is needed. If in doubt, add salt and white pepper.

Heat some oil (it will need to be a high-heat variety such as canola or peanut) in a large frying pan over medium-high heat. Start frying the gyoza so the bottoms are looking brown. Pour a small amount of water into the pan and cover tightly right away. Cook for 8-10 minutes or until gyozas are cooked through, the water has evaporated and the base of the dumplings are golden and can be lifted from the pan. The gyoza dough will be moist and chewy.

Quickly mix together these items in a little bowl to make a dipping sauce, in proportions entirely to your taste:

Rice vinegar
Chopped garlic
Chile powder
Sugar
Soy sauce

*Sometimes I make my own dough, it's easy, it just adds more time. I recommend the Extra Chewy Dough version of the Basic Dumpling Dough recipe from *Asian Dumplings* by Andrea Nguyen.

My Own Pork Pozole

High-intensity flavors in this stew.

INGREDIENTS

450-650 grams of pork shoulder or pork that has been kindly labeled "pork for pozole," cut into cubes

2 large dried ancho chilies, soaked in very hot water for 15 minutes, then seeded and rinsed
3 garlic cloves, peeled and chopped
1 large white onion, chopped

1 tablespoon cumin powder
1/2-1 teaspoon black pepper
1 teaspoon Spanish paprika
2 tablespoons red pepper flakes
1 teaspoon Mexican oregano
1 tablespoon salt

3-4 cups already-soaked and boiled dried pozole corn (the leftover boiled purple corn from Peruvian *chicha morada* can be good—*if* you have the time) or canned hominy, drained and rinsed
3-5 cups chicken broth

4-5 whole fresh jalapenos, chopped and seeded
2-3 large fresh pasilla chilies, seeded and stemmed

SOME SASSY GARNISHES

Limes (cut in wedges)
Sliced fresh radishes
Fresh chopped cilantro
Finely shredded cabbage
Corn tortillas, fresh
Corn tortillas, fried
Maybe some sliced avocados

DIRECTIONS

Place the meat in a large saucepan over medium heat, stir until brown, then cover with a little water.

In the meantime, soak the chilies, chop the onion, peel the garlic, chop the garlic cloves, etc. Chop the rinsed chilies and get your corn poised for action.

Add the spices to the meat! Don't forget the salt! Stir!

Add your veggie bits and broth to the meat stuff. Bring to a boil over medium heat, skim off any spooky looking foam. Reduce the heat, cover and simmer for about two hours*, checking and stirring to keep it from burning. Add water when needed to keep the consistency as you prefer. It should be more of a stew than a soup.

When you feel the two hours is up, take it off the stove to cool. Salt to taste (it may require quite a lot of salt—this is a key lesson I learned in Mexico).

After it cools down completely in the fridge, scrape as much fat off the top that you can. But hey if you love pork fat, don't.

Warm it up again when you're ready to serve. Any remaining pork fat will melt back into the broth.

Apply garnishes liberally at serving time, to your taste.

*Yes, two hours. This is to make the pork as soft and pull-aparty as possible. You could go longer than two hours, too, but I'll leave that up to you.

3 AFTERNOONS

When you have a look here, you're going to say, hey, how dare I slip dessert-esque and other sweet items in between lunch and dinner! Perhaps it has something to do with a vague Anglo-Saxon need for a tea time, or a pick-me-up dunch/linner meal? Or is it maybe because it's Sunday afternoon and you know you don't have anything better to do?

I developed my ice cream recipes from a variety of other recipes that I have tested over the years. I know you're going to think maybe you don't need the alcohol in these recipes but *please* leave it in for both texture and flavor. You might also wonder, why whole eggs in ice cream? Because using just egg yolks tastes nasty to me.

Normally I am a big fan of drinking just water, but sometimes I'll make a special drink. Both fruity drinks included here are special, but as I say in the recipe, only make the *chicha morada* if you're feeling like killing some serious time.

The Greek brioche bread and drunken figs come from years of experimentation and listening to various chefs talk about their obsessive approaches to these items. Both items have been popular with neighbors and friends.

The silly cookie recipes included are the results of experimentations with gluten free baking that led to me realizing I tend to prefer the texture of beans in cookies over the boring texture of plain all-purpose flour. If you consider Japanese desserts, you'll find a similar general trend in bean usage, although my (barbaric) approach is nothing like how Japanese desserts elevate beans.

Dear Gluten,

I'm sorry, I still love you.

But things are just different with beans.

--Me

"In My Own Dojo" Ice Cream

You absolutely may ***not*** skip the fruit preserves *or* the marsala.

INGREDIENTS

½ cup sugar
4 whole large eggs
2 cups heavy cream
2 cups whole milk

2 whole vanilla beans, split
2 tablespoons fruit preserves (apricot or sour cherry are a good place to start)
3 tablespoons marsala wine

DIRECTIONS

Heat cream, milk and split vanilla pods in heavy saucepan over medium heat, stir.

Meanwhile, use handheld mixer to beat eggs together, add the sugar to the eggs, beat until frothy.

When the cream/milk begins to bubble, take off heat and, with hand mixer running, add a bit of the cream/milk to the eggs. Very slowly continue adding just a little bit at a time to the eggs and sugar until you've added about 1 ½ cups. Now put the saucepan back on the burner, and with the mixer running, slowly pour everything back into the pot. This process is called tempering the eggs—look it up if you think you're going to be making custard or custard-based ice creams much.

When all is well combined, lose the mixer and stir with a heavy spoon, heating and stirring until the mixture is thickened enough to coat the back of the spoon and look especially attractive.

Remove from heat, cool for 15 minutes. Remove vanilla bean*, scrape out seeds, put seeds back into the milk-cream. Stir in marsala and fruit preserves thoroughly. Now push the mixture through a fine kitchen sieve, pushing and scraping with a spoon or a metal ladle to get everything through (this gives it a smoother texture and assuming your fruit preserves contain fruit as they should, it keeps any fruit skins or seeds out of the finished product).

Cool another 15 min.

Refrigerate overnight. The next day, churn it in an ice cream maker.

When it looks like ice cream that you want to eat, scrape it out and eat it! Or be prudent and freeze it in shallow containers.

If it does somehow freeze up slightly harder than you'd like, just let it sit on the kitchen counter for a while (15-20 minutes?) to soften up before scooping. Refreezing it after it's been out of the freezer for 15 minutes or whatever will almost always be fine because you haven't used a bunch of odd chemicals to stabilize it. The word on the street is that it's all that weird stuff that makes cheap ice cream go yucky after a little melting.

*Top secret hint: you can wash these vanilla beans off thoroughly and throw it in a little jar with some rum to make vanilla extract (or just some tasty rum).

Persian Ice Cream

I went to Persia and all I didn't get was this amazing ice cream.

INGREDIENTS

4 large whole eggs
1 cup white sugar
2 cups whole milk
2 cups heavy whipping cream
½ teaspoon excellent quality saffron, crushed then soaked in a spoonful of very hot milk
Sprinkle of sea salt
½ teaspoon mastic gum*, ground
1 teaspoon rose extract
3 tablespoons vodka (theoretically optional but this helps the ice cream stay soft and be easier to scoop so I strongly recommend *not* skipping it)
1 cup shelled high-quality pistachio nuts, roughly chopped

DIRECTIONS

In a small and appropriately deep mixing bowl, beat the eggs with the sugar with a hand mixer until smooth and foamy. Set aside.

In a large thick-bottomed pot on medium heat, slowly heat the milk and cream just to boiling while stirring. Continue to cook on low heat, constantly stirring.

Very carefully and very slowly, pour some the hot milk/cream mixture into the eggs and sugar. After you have added about half of the hot milk/cream to the eggs and sugar, it's OK to pour everything into the pot, just please blend it rapidly with the hand mixer right in the pot on the stovetop (now you see why it's a hand mixer and not a stand mixer). This process is called tempering the eggs—look it up if you think you're going to be making custard or custard-based ice creams much.

Continue heating the mixture on low heat while stirring constantly. It will start to get thickened (it should look like melted ice cream [!] and will coat a heavy spoon).

Take off the heat. Cool for a few minutes. Add the rose extract, alcohol, and soaked saffron/milk, then stir very well. Pour the custard mixture into a clean bowl, pouring it through a strainer to catch the bits of saffron and mastic gum crumbles** (or any egg bits that cooked too fast, shhh), then refrigerate until well chilled. Chilling all day or overnight is a good bet.

Churn in a home ice cream maker, adding pistachios after the first ten minutes or so, when it is firming up but not completely done yet. Eat immediately or freeze in shallow containers!

*It's worth investing in a little jar of mastic gum, it doesn't go bad and adds to the texture and flavor!

**These crumbles may stick to your strainer indefinitely. Get used to them.

Chicha Morada (Peruvian Purple Corn Drink)

For millennia, man has wondered, how can I use up all this purple corn and how can I literally spend days doing it? Finally, here is a fun and tasty way to use up your excess of purple corn *and* kill a perfectly good weekend.

INGREDIENTS

4 cups dried purple corn
1 large whole pineapple—peel, core, everything but the leaves, chopped
4 whole cloves
1 large green or yellow apple* (any cooking apple is OK), chopped
1 (real, "Ceylon") cinnamon stick
10-16 cups of water

4 large limes, juiced (you just want the juice here, sorry, peels)
1 cup of sugar or *piloncillo* palm sugar (maybe more less, depends on you), made into simple syrup**

DIRECTIONS

Soak the purple corn overnight in at least 10 cups of water in a large pot.

In the morning, boil the purple corn in its pot of water for about an hour (crank the heat high to boil and then turn it down a bit once you've brought it to a full boil). You might need to gently boil for maybe two or three hours, depending on the age and quality of the corn. Keep adding more water as needed! A lot of the purple color will go into the water and the corn will become chewable and then finally cooked and still-chewy but quite edible, like al dente pasta. Scoop out the edible corn kernels and keep them for making pork pozole (ah ha!). Refrigerate the purple water.

In another pot, put the apple, pineapple and cinnamon with enough water to cover. Bring to a boil, then cook gently on medium low for about an hour, stirring to prevent sticking—it's going to be pretty squishy. Add a little more water. Simmer on the lowest possible heat for about another 45 minutes. Keep stirring every now and then to prevent burning, add more water to keep things juicy and barely cooking.

Take the cooked fruit stuff off the stovetop. Combine it with your purple water and refrigerate it all together overnight. In the morning, carefully strain out all the remaining fruit bits and spices.

Add the lime juice, and add the simple syrup bit by bit. Adjust the sweetness as you prefer. Chill it.

Finally, drink it! Try it iced or not, as you like, plain or perhaps along with more fresh pineapple bits or your favorite Peruvian yummies (hey, do your own research on that).

*Quince is awesome in here instead of an apple, I recommend trying that if you have access to them. Here in Seattle many people have quince trees and don't even know what they are— snort! Pick them!

**Simple syrup: It's just a 1:1 ratio of water to sugar, boiled, stirred so the sugar dissolves, then cooled.

Inexact Watermelon-Ade Smoothie

INGREDIENTS

A really ripe watermelon
Fresh ginger
Simple syrup*
Limes or lemons—juice and zest
Lots of ice cubes
Salt

DIRECTIONS

Scoop all the fruit out of the watermelon. Don't worry about the seeds. Put all the watermelon fruit in a blender with enough water. Blend it up nice and mushy. Push it through a strainer to get the seeds and stuff out. Take a break and eat all the strained-out bits, seeds and all, for a nice fresh fruity fiber blast.

Put the watermelon juice/slush into a big pitcher. Add simple syrup to taste. Stir in as much fresh grated ginger as you think will taste good. Zest a few limes or lemons or some of both. Stir in about two or three limes' worth of their juice and all their zest. Taste. Throw a bunch of ice cubes in there. You may want to add more simple sugar since you know the ice cubes will melt and dilute the flavor a bit.

Now you can throw in a just pinch of salt to intensify the flavor. Stir and serve!

*Simple syrup: It's just a 1:1 ratio of water to sugar, boiled, stirred so the sugar dissolves, then cooled.

My Own "Greek" Sweet Brioche Braid

This makes one big loaf but you can divide into smaller portions and make little loaves— it's up to you.

The starting point concept for this bread is Greek tsoureki. Perhaps the addition of candied fruit to the recipe and the total amount of sugar make it less authentically Greek because it's more decadent than tsoureki, but the mahlepi and mastic keep it Greek enough for a neophyte's tastes.

Use a scale in this recipe for best results, especially for the flour, sugar and milk!! You could also weigh the smaller tidbits but even I find that tedious.

INGREDIENTS

Dough
500 grams bread flour
113 grams (½ cup) cold unsalted butter, cut into small cubes
168 grams (3 large) eggs (plus 1 more egg for later for brushing loaf after rising)
4 teaspoons instant yeast
183 grams (¾ cup) warm whole milk

Flavorings
100 grams (½ cup) sugar
¼ teaspoon mahlepi (also called mahleb)
¼ teaspoon mastic gum, crushed fine
¼ teaspoon liquid almond extract
¼ teaspoon cinnamon
1 teaspoon salt
¼ teaspoon orange blossom water

Dried Fruits
2-4 tablespoons candied citrus, diced fine
2-4 tablespoons golden raisins

DIRECTIONS

Mix as you would brioche (I recall that *Bon Appetit* has published an online article called *Brioche Made Easy* so I don't feel the need to add four more pages to this recipe), in a quality stand mixer, for at least 15 minutes, using the dough hook for the latter part to get the dough kneaded nicely. As with brioche, it's gonna look nasty as you go along through this process, just don't mind it and plunge forward, trusting your proper weighing of the ingredients, knowing that it'll get silky and perfect after it has been hooked enough. (Note! The dough will still feel sticky even when it's perfect, so please don't add more flour.) Hook in the flavorings, including the sugar, last and give it another 5 minutes of slow kneading to incorporate. Putting the sugar in at this point is supposedly giving the gluten time to form strands without sugar in the way, so you get a nicer bready texture in the end. If you put the sugar in at the beginning, the bread will have a different, sloppier texture (sorry, don't they say read the recipes through a couple of times before getting started?). Don't fret, though, as the taste will be the same.

Turn dough into a generously buttered bowl and turn dough around to grease it up all over with the butter. Cover top of bowl well with plastic wrap to keep the happiness inside. Rise 1 hour in your cozy kitchen.

After an hour, you'll see the dough has expanded delightfully. Slap in the chopped dried fruits, as thoroughly as possible. Punch dough down, flip over, really smush those fruits in. Cover bowl again with the wrap, cover the whole shebang with a dish towel to make yourself feel homey, and refrigerate overnight.

After refrigeration is where you'll see the texture looking and feeling great: soft, workable, dreamy, and not sticky. Punch it down. To make one giant loaf, cut into three equal pieces (Weigh it! Do the math and divide— unless you are an experienced great Greek grandma, if you "eyeball it" the loaves will be uneven and may bake up unevenly!).

Roll as neatly as possible (I struggle with this, but the neater the better) into three logs about an inch thick and 14 inches long. On a half sheet baking pan with a silicon liner or parchment paper, shape into a braid and tuck the ends firmly under.

Lightly cover with plastic wrap and then a clean dishtowel. Rise 90 minutes or more (could be 2 hours, depending on the temperature in your kitchen) until it appears to have doubled in size. You can also let it rise in the fridge overnight and bake in the morning— in that case, you probably need to let it sit at room temp for *at least* one full hour before baking, though. However, your local atmospheric conditions have an impact on the rising, so use your brain and observe the rising behavior of the dough.

Preheat oven to 350°F.

When the loaf is completely risen (that means it *doesn't* pop back when you poke it boldly; it doesn't pop back because the yeast have let out as much gas as they can and will soon be on the decline), brush it gently all over with a well-beaten egg, then top with a generous sprinkling of chopped/sliced almonds and coarse sugar right down the middle. Do this only if you want—it is not necessary, but it looks and tastes great. Note that the loaf will expand in the oven, so you can pile the toppings right along the center and they'll spread out as the bread expands more in the oven.

Bake about 50-60 minutes on the middle rack of the oven. It should be dark golden brown when it's done, so keep an eye on it and know you may need more time. If you're worried about it getting too dark, have a piece of aluminum foil ready to tent over the bread at about 30-35 minutes. Use your best judgement! Heck, make it a few times if you don't get it right the first time, who's going to complain?

Remember that if you make smaller loaves, they're going to take less time to bake, and brown faster, etc. Usually about 45 minutes is good. Let rest on a rack until cool before slicing.

Makes killer French toast!!

Many Options Drunken Figs

I love figs. Here is one fun thing you can do with your figgy friends that will give you a lot of spine-tingling options.

INGREDIENTS

Perfectly ripe flawless figs of any sweet variety
Bottle of tasty spirits/liquor/liqueur of your choice (such as brandy)
Sugar (about ¼ cup per cup of figs)
1 vanilla bean (per jar)

DIRECTIONS
Wash and cut a lot of figs into quarters. Eat some. Keep your little paws clean. Put the clean cut figs in just a bit of water in a pot with the sugar. Cook for about 10-20 minutes on medium heat until the figs are soft but not complete mush. Scoop out the figs with a slotted spoon and put them into sterilized glass jars, almost up to the top but give the jar space at the top. Take a vanilla bean, split it in half with a knife, and put it in each jar too. Cook the figgy syrup gently on medium heat in the pot to get it obviously thicker, and more syrupy, than it was, perhaps 10-20 minutes (maybe longer), depending on the amount of water you started with. Pour it over the cooked figs in the jars. Now fill the jars to the very, very top with tasty brandy. That brandy is to keep the figs fully submerged. Put the jars in the refrigerator for a long time (two weeks to a month is usually pretty good). The brandy and sugar will soak into the figs and preserve them. Eat them until they are gone. They are unlikely to "go bad" before you finish them up but be sure to keep them refrigerated; and they'll probably be OK for 3-6 months.

IDEAS

These figs will taste excellent on vanilla ice cream.

I like to chop them up and bake them inside empanadas with ricotta and goat cheese, a dash of salt and a little raw sugar or top-quality honey.

Excellent on dessert pizza (with cultured butter, mascarpone cheese, candied citrus, a sprinkle of turbinado sugar and a few gratings of nutmeg) as well.

You could experiment with different kinds of brandy or you could use other tasty spirit/liqueur like amaretto, rum, Grand Marnier or kirschwasser, it depends on your flavor interests and curiosity. I don't recommend flavorless alcohols or beers...not especially tasty...just think about it...

Highly Versatile Beany Chocolate Chip Cookies

Just happens to be gluten free.

INGREDIENTS

<u>Moisty Bits</u>
2 generous cups of homemade boiled beans (red, chickpea, black), with their associated liquid (no need to rinse after their final boil)
2 eggs (or 2 teaspoons meringue powder or 1 egg or use 2 "eggs" of Egg Replacer if you like, or look for "flax eggs" mentioned on page 65)
¼ cup creamy peanut butter or other nut butter (hazelnut butter is the bomb if you can find it)
2 tablespoons coconut oil, softened (not essential but yummy)
¼ cup butter, softened (feel free to replace with coconut oil)
2 teaspoons vanilla extract
¼ cup molasses
1-2 tablespoons raw (turbinado) sugar
20 drops liquid stevia (or ¼ cup sugar or some other sweetener if you're a stevia-phobe)

<u>Dry-y Bits</u>
1 teaspoon salt
1 teaspoon baking powder
¼ cup teff flour
¼ cup coconut flour
1 tablespoon tapioca flour
¼ cup instant oatmeal (optional)

1-2 cups chocolate chips or chopped chocolate of your choice
½ - 1 cup sliced or chopped nuts of your choice (optional)

DIRECTIONS

SOME of EACH

Pulverize the moisty bits hard in food processor or mash very, very well with a potato masher or ricer. Mix the dry-y bits in a separate bowl. Add moisty bits to dry-y bits and hope real hard for the best, then stir. *It should seem pretty similar to "regular" cookie dough.*

Spoon small spoonfuls of this goop onto a cookie sheet lined with silicone liner or parchment paper. Top them with some of the chocolate chips artfully, if possible. Note that if you don't make them look cosmetically good now, they may look like doo-doo later because they will not flatten out as they bake.

Bake in center of oven at 375°F for 12-17ish minutes.

*Make this chocolate-chocolate chip by replacing ¼ cup of the flour with ¼ cup cocoa. It is OK with me if you remove/replace any ingredients that offend you, but do so with a sense of curiosity as opposed to highly specific expectations.

Just Yummy (Banana Peanut Butter Chocolate Chip Cookies)

Another silly cookie recipe full of wacky tidbits! And possibly gluten free if you have some gluten free flours hanging around your pantry.

INGREDIENTS

<u>Moisty Bits</u>
1 large overripe banana
2 large eggs
½ cup butter
3 tablespoons cream cheese
¼ cup peanut butter
1 vanilla bean worth of vanilla seeds (save bean pod for making vanilla sugar or extract)
¼ cup brown sugar
3 tablespoons blackstrap molasses

<u>Dry-y Bits</u>
1 cup coconut flour
1 cup white whole wheat flour (you could try a combination of teff and brown rice to make this gluten free)
1 teaspoon salt
1 teaspoon baking soda
⅓ cup oatmeal

1 cup roughly chopped top quality dark chocolate

DIRECTIONS

Mix wet well, then add dry stuff. Bake at 375°F for 12 minutes. Slurp.

4 EVENINGS

Alrighty, this final section is about the things that we know we should probably be eating in the evening, even though we don't always choose these things. I know that the evening is the time that I will work on finishing up all the afternoon desserts. Do with it what you will.

What we have here are a few worthwhile salads, pizzas and soups. I will be quick to say that I have an extreme distaste for cutting and preparing vegetables for salads. Yet I believe the salady items included here are worthwhile enough to cut vegetables for, so that is saying something. I think the use of a good quality box grater and a mandolin for preparing vegetables have helped me preserve a tiny shred (no pun intended, but keeping it anyway) of sanity in the kitchen.

You will see there are several pizza-like recipes in this section. That is because it is inevitable that someone in your household, particularly you, will want to eat pizza in the evening. I recommend following your recommendations in this regard.

I only have two soup recipes to share right now because the *SOUP TO END ALL SOUPS* recipe could lead you down so many paths of soups, why waste my currently very limited and precious finger strength trying to explain all the additional options? Finally, the *Lazy-Healthy-Easy Soup Cheat* is what you could have late at night if you have already had too much of one of the pizzas or ice cream dishes but you would still like to virtuously stuff your little gullet with the wholesome and savory goodness of vegetables.

Red Cabbage Goodness

This is very good the next day except the flavonoids (good stuff, they say) from the cabbage will have turned everything a tawdry pink color.

INGREDIENTS

Veggies

½ one large red cabbage
1 head of broccoli, with stem and leaves

6 colorful mini peppers
¼ cup chopped green onion *or* ¼ cup diced shallots

Dressing

1 clove garlic, chopped
Juice of 1 lemon
3 tablespoons olive oil
2 tablespoons sour cream
1 teaspoon sugar
1 teaspoon of garlic salt
¼ cup fresh Italian flat leaf parsley, chopped fine*

DIRECTIONS

Using a mandolin, very thinly slice cabbage into a large mixing bowl. Chop the head of broccoli into very small pieces. Use the broccoli stems, too—just peel them and dice them up. *And* the leaves, just cut in a chiffonade style. Cut bell pepper into small strips or rings. Chop up the shallots or dice the green onions. If you opt for green onions, it's OK to use some of the green, but don't use too much (it gets tough at the top).

Put all the dressing stuff into a small jar with a tight lid and shake until combined.

Pour the dressing over the salad and mix well until all the veggies are evenly coated. Serve at *room temperature*. I am so tired of ice-cold salads.

*Try any other fresh herbs that you suspect might be tasty if you have them on hand. Dill? Cilantro?

Shalloty Goodness Salad Dressing

Great on greens. Great greens, *not* sub-par greens. Thanks for listening.

INGREDIENTS

1 generous pinch brown or white sugar
1 teaspoon kosher salt
½ teaspoon white pepper
3 tablespoons very finely minced shallots
1 very finely minced clove of garlic
1 tablespoon mustard*
½ cup top-notch extra virgin olive oil
¼-½ cup red wine vinegar
½-1 teaspoon herb of choice** (optional)

DIRECTIONS

Put everything together in a small jar with a tight lid. Close lid and shake vigorously. Taste. Adjust seasonings if needed.

Pour over greens of your choice. I like this on room-temperature arugula and *in-season* halved cherry tomatoes (or homemade oven-dried cherry tomatoes, yum). Grind some black pepper over the top; maybe throw on some great freshly grated parmesan cheese, etc.

*Try hot Chinese mustard if you're feeling bold.

**Thyme? Tarragon? You choose what seems good, it's optional.

Spanish Lentil-Parsley Salad

Most lentil salads are too heavy on the lentils for my tastes. This one is happier due to its proportions being more on the parsley side.

INGREDIENTS

1 cup dry Spanish (brown) lentils
1 bay leaf
1 teaspoon salt

Raw veggies
Entire celery heart, diced or sliced
2 full bunches parsley, washed and chopped very small (stems and all)
¾ cup very finely sliced or shredded carrots
¾ cup red onion or shallot, diced very fine

Dressing
4 cloves garlic, minced
½ teaspoon dried thyme
3 tablespoons sumac
1 teaspoon celery seed
1 ½ teaspoon salt
1 teaspoon ground black pepper
¼ cup olive oil
3 tablespoons apple cider vinegar

DIRECTIONS

In a saucepan add enough water to rinsed lentils to cover by 1 inch. Add bay leaf. Bring to boil, reduce heat and simmer uncovered for about 20 minutes or until lentils are tender but not mushy (this is a delicate place – ask yourself, would I want to eat this?).

Drain lentils, remove bay leaf, cool them down to room temperature. Stir in salt.

Make the dressing by adding the dressing ingredients to a jar and shaking vigorously.

Combine lentils, carrots, onion. Stir in chopped parsley with your hands. Pour on the dressing. Toss to mix, add more salt if needed, and serve at room temperature.

NOTE

If you have really amazing in-season tomatoes floating around, they'd probably go alongside this nicely, just sliced and salted/peppered.

Sri Lankan Carrot Salad

Sri Lankans don't seem to eat copious amounts of "salad" but they do eat a lot of "sambol." I think you can get sneaky and make a salad-sambol hybrid. Here is a shot at that.

INGREDIENTS

3 cups finely grated carrots, juice squeezed out (with your hands)
1 large red shallot, sliced very thinly
2 cups grated fresh coconut*
4 Thai mouse turd chilies**, finely chopped
1-2 cloves garlic, peeled and chopped
1 teaspoon cumin, toasted and ground
1 tablespoon ground Maldive fish chips† (or 1 tablespoon fish sauce)
Juice of one small lime
Grated rind of the lime (just the green part)
1 teaspoon red chili powder
1 teaspoon sugar
1 teaspoon salt

Fresh coriander to decorate, if you like (keep the leaves whole and chop the stems small for a snappy presentation)

DIRECTIONS

Dump all the ingredients in a bowl and stir together! Adjust flavorings. If it's bland, you might go for more of the Maldive fish/fish sauce. Add the optional fresh coriander just when serving.

*Asian groceries sell fresh grated coconut in frozen packets. Great stuff to use for this— a serious time saver.

**Yes, this is a real thing.

†Dried Skipjack tuna rocks, in a nutshell, for a uniquely Sri Lankan umami blast. Fish sauce is an OK substitute but you can order Maldive fish online so you don't have a ton of excuses.

EXCITING VARIATIONS

You might try this with rainbow carrots for visual stimulation. Or break out of that ever-confining carrot box and try making the whole thing with raw beets instead.

Yum Sin (Noodle Salad), My Way

This is a Thai recipe for spicy glass noodle salad and I've discovered that in a pinch you can also make it with al dente ramen noodles.

INGREDIENTS

4 bundles of glass noodles (also called "bean threads") or 2 packages of instant ramen noodles (without their spice packets)

1 tablespoon canola oil
2 small sliced shallots
1 tablespoon chopped garlic
1 tablespoon fish sauce (*not* optional)
Juice of one lime
3 Thai mouse turd chilies*, chopped small
½ teaspoon sugar
½ cup whole cilantro leaves and finely chopped stems
½ cup yellow cherry or pear tomatoes, sliced in half
Some peanut oil
½ cup diced pan-fried** fresh tofu
¼ cup roughly chopped roasted peanuts
½ cup finely sliced Chinese or regular celery
¼ cup Thai style dried shrimp, pan fried (optional)
Red pepper flakes

DIRECTIONS

To prepare the glass noodles soak them in very hot water until they are completely clear (this should take about 6-8 minutes if you let it go longer they can get mushy so please keep an eye on them). Take the noodles out of the hot water and rinse them with cold water, then drain. Chop them up on a cutting board.

To make the ramen noodles, just boil the noodle bricks (toss the spice packets!) about 1-2 minutes until al dente and pull them out of the water, rinse with cold water, drain, and chop them up on a cutting board.

Whatever noodle you decide to use, preparing the rest of the stuff is easy! Except you have to cut or fry or slice or chop it all separately, sorry. But then you just plop it all in a bowl and then add the cool noodles to that.

You may want to add a little more sugar to the mixture, or a little more fish sauce or possibly more lime juice. It depends on your flavor preferences. Also, note that some people will fry the garlic before they add it to the salad, and that is nice. Some people also insist on frying the roasted peanuts. You might also toss in a little bit of peanut oil to keep everything slick if that seems good.

You can top the salad with more cilantro to make it look pretty. You can add more veggies as you like. Some people also add cooked ground pork or chicken.

Serve with extra red pepper flakes for the spice lovers.

*Yes, this is a real thing.

**Hey, it is super, super easy to pan fry tofu. Just cut fresh extra firm tofu into small cubes and fry in a little bit of canola oil in a nonstick frying pan on medium heat, while salting and turning/stirring it so that most of the sides of the tofu gets brown. Boom.

Sourdough Pizza Dough for a Crowd

Originally, I thought this pizza dough should be kneaded but it's not necessary, really. You still get a nice but tender dough.

Note that this is a hard core multiple day trip! Even so, you are free to start in the morning and then attempt to bake in the evening. But for a sexier sourdough taste, go for the all-day then overnight fridge fermentation plus 2-3 more days of fermentation in the fridge.

I say this is for a crowd because I host pizza-making parties and this is a decent amount of dough for 8-10 people to make individual sized pizzas together (more than 1.5+ kg of dough).

INGREDIENTS
(Sloppy measures—feel free to convert to grams if you're feisty but it is not worthwhile as this recipe isn't so precise.)

3 cups room temperature sourdough starter*
1-2 tablespoons of your favorite olive oil
2-3 teaspoons honey
1 teaspoon yeast mixed with 1 tablespoon warm water, just to dissolve
2-2½ teaspoons sea salt
3 cups high-gluten Italian pizza flour (or just regular bread flour)

1-4 *more* cups high-gluten pizza flour, depending on your sourdough starter consistency
A splash of olive oil for the rising bowl/container
½ cup or so of whole wheat flour for your countertop when shaping the pizzas
½ cup or so of medium grind cornmeal or polenta for sprinkling on your baking pans (or stone)

DIRECTIONS

In the morning, in a pretty large bowl, begin to create the dough by stirring the yeast-water into your sourdough starter, then add the honey and olive oil. Cup by cup, gradually add the first 3 cups of flour. Mix with a fat spoon until it's combined. Cover with plastic wrap and let it hang out on your countertop all day. In the evening, gradually stir in the additional flour, adding more flour until you have a dough that you can handle well enough so it doesn't stick to your hands badly—it will be sticky but not unbearably sticky.

Don't bother kneading it. Before you sleep, stir it, then put in the fridge, overnight.

In the morning, give it a good stir, smash out any gas, put it back in the refrigerator for 2-3 days. During that time, admire it daily and punch it down to let a maximum number of yeast farts out. It won't rise much. If you won't be baking it by the third day, divide it into balls the size you like (perhaps 180-200 grams is a nice size—that gives you a 10-inch crust). Wrap each ball in plastic wrap and freeze. You can slowly thaw any number of frozen balls in the refrigerator starting in the morning of the day when you will bake in the evening.

SHAPING AND BAKING

Put rack at very bottom of oven. If you have a pizza stone** that you don't just always leave in the oven (which I do because I have nowhere else to keep it), please make sure it's in there. You certainly can't just toss it in there later when the oven is already hot—it will break!

Preheat oven to 500-525 °F. Use a separate thermometer in your oven so you know it's really at that temperature—most ovens don't have great built-in thermostats and will claim that the oven is at the correct temperature when it's not even close yet.

Allow dough to rest on the countertop at room temperature for about 30 minutes.

Shape the dough on a clean (duh) surface sprinkled generously with whole wheat flour. The general advice is that you work by turning and stretching the dough with your fingertips, as you shape it, working from the center of the dough to the outside edge. Imagine the pizzeria guy tossing the pizza, and you're doing the same action on your countertop. Don't stress about the pizza being a perfect circle and don't wad it up and try to start over (this will not help and you will need to let it rest again). The dough is still going to be slightly sticky and floppy but just be patient with it and use the flour and keep working until it looks like a thickness you like and/or it fits the size of your pan or stone.

Place dough on an oiled perforated pizza pan that has been lightly coated with medium grind cornmeal or polenta. Brush the top of the crust all over with olive oil. Add your toppings!

Bake in the hot oven on the stone (yes, put your metal pan on your stone) until browned and toppings appear cooked (5-7 minutes, typically).

It's OK to top the pizza with a splash of more olive oil when it comes out of the oven if that seems like a good idea.

*Try *Wild Grape Starter* from Allrecipes.com if you can't get your hands on any starter from me or from a friend. Then you will need to give yourself around 9-10 days before the dough is ready, but when you have your own starter, you can keep it going as long as you want. If you make this pizza often, you can make somewhat large batches of starter and not "throw the excess away" (common sourdough starter advice) because you will use so much of it just for this recipe.

**If you have a pizza stone, use it. If you don't have one, don't cry, just make the pizza on a metal sheet that you've oiled and sprinkled with medium grind cornmeal. What's great about a metal baking sheet (preferably perforated, designed for pizza, but a plain old oiled cookie sheet works fine, too) is that your crowd of pizza-making newbs won't be flopping raw pizzas backwards or sideways straight onto the pizza stone and making a delightfully smoky mess of your stone and oven. You can also add toppings in a much more leisurely fashion when you use a metal sheet of some kind. This is because if you use a pizza peel to put the pizza straight on a stone, you need to move quickly to prevent the dough from sticking to the surface of the peel. Waiting 30 minutes for someone to "cut the vegan cheese" while the dough becomes more and more attached to the peel will *not* a happy pizza peel (or smoke detector) make.

Whole Potato Pizza Crusts

Makes just two large but somehow measly "crust"-like disks …WTH! Let me know later if this is worth the effort.

INGREDIENTS

400 grams of starchy type potatoes, washed and unpeeled, but chopped small
¼ cup warm water (about 110°F)
2 teaspoons honey
2 teaspoons active dry yeast
1 ½ cups white rice flour
½ teaspoon xanthan gum
¼-½ cup tapioca starch*
¾ teaspoon kosher salt

1 "flax egg": stir and rest 5 minutes:
    1 tablespoon golden flaxseed meal
    2 ½ tablespoons water
1 tablespoon delicious olive oil
Plenty of additional delicious olive oil for oiling your baking surface
Some herbs (optional)**

Pizza toppings of your choice— in generous amounts!

DIRECTIONS

Boil unpeeled potatoes and cook until soft, about 25 minutes; remove from water. Mash them with a masher, a ricer or your fists of rage, it's up to you.

Stir together the warm water, honey and yeast in a measuring cup or small bowl. Let sit until foamy, typically just a few minutes. You're only waiting to make sure the yeast is alive and the foam will tell you it is.

Add the potatoes, rice flour, tapioca starch and salt to the bowl of a stand mixer. Mix on medium speed with the generic paddle attachment until the mixture is combined. Continuing to mix on medium, add the "flax egg," oil, yeast mixture and continue to mix until the dough comes together (it will be sticky but not horribly). Cover the bowl tightly with plastic wrap and set in a warm place to pretend to yourself that it is rising, maybe one hour. It won't really be rising in the conventional sense because there isn't gluten in this dough to trap the yeast fart bubbles, but it will kind of be fermenting and smelling nice.

Line two baking sheets with something very non-stick (parchment paper or a silicon mat). Oil that non-stick surface very, very generously with olive oil. Pat (it will *not* roll out, so don't bother trying) the dough into two thin-crust (¼ inch to ⅓ inch thick) pizza-like shapes. Bake at 400°F for about 15-20 minutes—or until they're firm and golden but not brown. Keep an eye on them, the length of time needed may vary! You want them to look dry and golden, like something you might eventually want to eat, you know.

Rest the baked crusts on a wire rack. Be sure to peel off your non-stick whatever-you-used carefully.

Now crank up the oven to 510-525°F.

Put each crust on a baking sheet sprinkled with cornmeal. Add your pizza toppings—be generous! Now bake until the toppings look cooked! Maybe 5-7 minutes. Watch closely to avoid burning! Consider giving the pizza a splash of excellent olive oil when it comes out of the oven, if you're into that kind of debauchery. I recommend eating these shortly you make them, as they get a bit cardboardy if they've been in the fridge for more than 3-4 days.

If you want to make these crusts ahead time, when they're completely cool and toppingless, wrap in whatever appropriate material you have (parchment, then aluminum foil?) then freeze.

You can pull them out later to bake right away as above with toppings— there's no need to thaw— but may need a few minutes more time (7-10ish minutes seems good) total in the oven. Keep your peepers on them.

*If you use less tapioca starch, they're more potatoey, so consider that. If you use more tapioca, they're more gluey and bready. Also, more xanthan gum will make it gummier, so be stingy with that stuff.

**How does rosemary in this feel? That'd be nice.

NOTE

It's OK to use an egg white instead of the flax egg if you're into that more than flax; it is also slightly less risky for newbs, as flax tends to add a little extra goo to the whole scene and can weigh the dough down.

Disconcerting Inverted Field Roast Pizza

Field Roast is a yummy vegetarian sausage with a great flavor. If that offends you, use real sausage, I'm not looking.

This isn't really pizza "dough" that goes on top but it does bake up as a reasonable facsimile of crust.

INGREDIENTS

Bottom
1 tablespoon olive oil
1 package of Italian style Field Roast, chopped up in small bits
1 cup yellow onion, diced
2 cups of pasta sauce of your choice (make your own or buy pre-made. Vodka sauce has been nice)
½ cup good quality green olives, stuffed with garlic, such as the Sicilian variety, sliced
1 teaspoon fish sauce
2 cups good quality mozzarella cheese, shredded

Top
2 eggs
1 cup skim milk
2 tablespoons tasty olive oil
½ cup all-purpose flour
½ cup white whole wheat flour
½ teaspoon baking powder
½ teaspoon salt
1 teaspoon sugar
½-1 teaspoon chopped fresh rosemary (optional)
¼ cup Parmesan cheese, grated
Sprinkling of medium grind cornmeal

DIRECTIONS

Preheat oven to 400°F.

Fry Field Roast and onion in the olive oil a large non-stick frying pan for about 10 minutes on medium heat. Add pasta sauce, olives and fish sauce, then simmer on medium low about 2 minutes. Remove from heat and pour sauce into a 9x13 inch glass baking dish. Sprinkle all over with mozzarella cheese.

In a nicely sized mixing bowl, whisk together eggs, milk and oil until blended. Whisk in flours, sugar, baking soda, salt and parmesan until blended but there's absolutely no need to over stir—as with pancakes, over-stirring will make this crust grumpy. Toss in the rosemary if you're into that. Pour this mixture over the sauce and stuff in the baking dish. Sprinkle a wee tad of cornmeal evenly on top.

Bake 25 minutes, or until the crust is golden brown. Let rest for at least 15-20 minutes before slicing and serving. Be prepared for things to get messy if you can't resist slicing into it. It's also going to become messier with additional toppings – consider this a feature rather than a bug and all will go well.

The kid says this makes excellent leftovers and is a nice lunchbox item wrapped in aluminum foil.

OPTIONS

Please add fried mushrooms, diced capers, roasted peeled red peppers, chopped fresh basil and other such things and give it a more vegetably boost.

A SOUP TO END ALL SOUPS

Versatile! Try it. But don't blame me.

INGREDIENTS

2 tablespoons olive oil
1 large white, red*, or yellow onion, diced
2-3 cloves garlic, diced
1 celery heart, sliced
6 carrots, sliced
2 bay leaves

Vegetables of your choice, such as:
½-1 head of green or red* cabbage, thinly sliced
2-4 spicy or mild peppers (bell peppers, jalapenos, poblano, Anaheim, Hungarian, etc.), chopped/diced
1-2 chayote squash, diced/cubed
8-12 cups of vegetable or chicken broth (or just water, as you prefer)

2-3 cups of beans, already fully cooked (such as from a can, or homemade). Any of these are good:
-Kidney
-Red
-Garbanzo
-Black
-Pinto
-Great Northern
1-2 cups of diced tomatoes (canned or fresh)

Spices that you like. I like:
1-2 tablespoons cumin, roasted and ground
1 tablespoon coriander, roasted and ground
1 tablespoon red pepper flakes
1 tablespoon oregano (fresh, chopped, or dried is fine)
1-2 teaspoons epazote (Mexican spice, OK to leave out)

1 teaspoon white pepper
1 tablespoon coarsely ground black pepper
SALT, to taste (could be a lot, like 2-3 tablespoons—don't be surprised)

If you like, also add, at the very, very end:
1-2 cups (or more) already fully cooked chicken, cut in cubes or pulled with a fork
1-2 cups already fully cooked and cubed firm red or yellow potatoes (*no* Russet potatoes, they turn into mush)
1-2 cups already fully cooked rice, any kind (I prefer red) or other grain (quinoa, millet or amaranth are nice)
Extra frozen vegetables (there's no shame!) such as corn and/or spinach
Any amount of well-diced fresh cilantro or Italian flat leaf parsley (best added at serving time)

DIRECTIONS

In an 8-quart (big) pot—or bigger:
Cook the garlic, onions, celery with the bay leaves and oil on medium-high heat. Add the carrots. Stir around a bit more until you see them softening. Throw all the rest of the cut-up vegetables in the second category into the pot. Add a cup or so of the broth to steam it along. Stir—you'll see it's cooking by steaming. Put a lid on it for a few minutes. Have a peek to see if things are softening up. When you can see they're getting softer, add the rest of the broth, and bring everything to a boil.

When it boils, those veggies should look like they're getting cooked nicely but not getting over-cooked. Now turn the heat down to medium-low and add beans and spices. Taste and add plenty of salt as you go along. Simmer for 20 minutes. Add tomatoes. Simmer another 10 minutes.

The soup is probably done now. If not, simmer for another 30 minutes or so.

Now you can add the other things (cooked meat, rice, potatoes, etc.) and anything else that you think might be tasty. Think of this soup as a nice way to use up leftovers.

Note that if you decide to add rice or grains to it at the end, you'll likely need to add more broth or water, as even cooked grains are going to soak up more soup liquid. Check the soup flavor. When in doubt, add more salt. Taste again.

After you let this cool, put it into containers and refrigerate. If you get tired of eating just the soup as-is, you can take out the bay leaves and put it into a blender for a creamy soup.

As the soup ages, it starts tasting better— and you can add things to it to stretch it out. It generally lasts me about a week.

For even more things to add to stretch it out, try adding more vegetables to it as the week goes along. I like to add heavily spiced oven roasted okra right at serving time (don't add before—it will get slimy). The easiest vegetable to add to extend the soup is chopped frozen spinach that you've nuked in the microwave with a splash of water.

When you extend the soup, remember to adjust with more broth and salt and pepper, maybe some hot sauce and garlic powder to keep the flavor balance groovy. Be sure to reheat until very hot.

You could potentially throw some cooked pasta into the soup when you're ready to serve (if you didn't put rice/grains in it yet). You could also drain off the broth and serve the chunky contents of soup over some pasta like a sauce. Or maybe blend the soup up, add oil and salt and cheese and/or oil to make it into a "creamy" pasta sauce? Or take that sauce and cook it down and use it as a sauce on your pizza? Let your taste buds guide your experiments.

If this soup turns out bland somehow, even with copious amounts of salt, consider throwing Creole seasoning and fried Andouille sausage on top or on the side—usually works like a charm.

*When you use red and purple veggies in your soup, note that your soup may be purplish-blue the next day—no worries!

Lazy-Healthy-Easy Soup Cheat

So easy, you'll scream...into your pillow at night.

INGREDIENTS

2-3 cups frozen greens (kale, frozen chard or frozen spinach)
1 can (any size, get crazy, or use your best judgement) black beans or pinto beans, rinsed*
Enough vegetable or chicken broth** to cover the above
½ teaspoon onion powder (if you have it around)
Salt and pepper to taste

Hot sauce of your choice

DIRECTIONS

Put everything except the hot sauce in a blender and blend, adding more broth until you like the consistency. Blend it for many minutes if you like things smooth. Blend it for a short while if you like a little chunk. If you're feeling crazy, run it through a food mill or press it through a sieve to get ultra-smooth (but note that as you do this, it becomes less and less "easy"). Microwave it all until very hot but you can cook it on the stovetop if you have time. Add more salt, pepper and then hot sauce to taste. Eat with rice or toast or whatever carbs you enjoy most.

*The canned beans that come with seasonings already in them can make this soup an even lazier good option—and no need to waste 30 seconds on the rinsing! Or, if you don't want to eat beans because you have a hot date lined up or perhaps just don't happen to have any beans around, just forget them and make this with only the greens.

**I like the bouillon paste stuff in a jar. Those who know say it's the place to go.

THE WRAP UP

Well, there you have it, we've fizzled out together and you've wasted some portion of your time having a look at these ideas and maybe even trying a few yourself. I hope you have found it entertaining as well as tasty, although I try not to be attached to specific outcomes. Let me know how you liked this one and stay tuned for more tomfoolery.

Made in the USA
San Bernardino, CA
15 February 2018